# *Wheel of Light*

## JAMES RANCE

THE BLACK STORK IS RISEN...

*JRance*

| | E | S | T | |
|---|---|---|---|---|
| A | C | I | D | |
| | 2 | 0 | 2 | 0 |
| B | A | T | H | |

**PUBLISHING**

First published in 2023 by Acid Bath Publishing
Sheffield, United Kingdom
www.acidbathpublishing.com

ISBN: 978-1-8381789-5-6

Poems © James Rance 2023
Edited and typeset by Paul Whelan
Artwork © James Rance 2023

Alternative versions of *The Rite*, "Vulparia", "Cornfield Annuals", and "Urticaria" first appeared in *Forge Zine* in 2020. *The Augur, The Haruspex,* and *The Wanderer* were featured in issues throughout 2020. Previous iterations of "Ritual of Abduction" and "Persephone" were published by *Forge Zine* in 2021.

Printed and bound in Great Britain by Imprint Digital

# Contents

## III. Autumn – *The Haruspex*

## IV. Winter – *The Wanderer*

in this state of reverie,
under the rain with sun in your eyes,

You saw *barbarians looking to the west,*
*barbarians leaving the forest,* *barbarians*
*marching to the* *west,*

An old man loaded down
*with a package of clouds on his back,*
a flower

in white lace, *its neck pierced by a stone.*

And if you die, are you not sure of being
roused from the dead?
You have no name.

Игорь Стравинский

Time falls,
the wheel turns,

The
Great
Rite
*begins* ...

when
mankind was a twinkle in a monkey's
eye,

after a day of biblical rainfall, up
from the ground appeared the
heads of automatons.

the 'Gas'
the towers of Babel,
*The antipode of the landscape.*
*A beautiful German girl.*

*The straits of Mars.*
*The absolute presence.*

Come, the spirit breathes outside the spirit.

I. Spring - *The Rite*

# Ritual of Abduction

death breathed gently upon the rite:
blistered,
taken by the wind.

the dawn of a year
split in two by a swelling bruise,
the grass bristled with dew.

the girl from the village
was taken up in strong arms
and led to the field

where the circle-dancers gathered their
skirts and joined their hands together,
their fingertips turned cold by
birdsong –

the girl from the village
was taken by the wind
and blown through the meadow,

over the bright hairs
of aster and cornflower,

through the bleeding

palm of the poppy anemone.

she raised her arms
to greet the red eye of the
sun, which wept above her,

and laughed until her jaw broke off.

# Clasping-leaf

on a mountain under the gaze of a blazing eye,
the rocks too hot to touch,
the dancers tied ribbons around
their arms, their hands, through their hair,
and formed their circles,

a wheel bound up in red
turning in the desert. far from here,
a man walks the bone-white crags,
follows a twisting path of stone.
he meditates beneath a marula tree,
sinks into visions of a white sun hidden
behind black wings, of barbarians crossing
the grassland,

a warlike virtue, a torrent of rain
summoned by the stamping feet of young girls –

the dancers beat the earth with their palms and scatter powdered dye,
move closer, tie themselves to the centre and contort their bodies.
the dancers burst and break themselves in half,
draw on their faces with painted sand –

as the wanderer returns from his otherworld,
a circle of red

bristling between the burnt fingers of the mountains

calls down a storm.

# Amphora

the ground is cracked and reddened
by dust
rich with flavour
bright things that sparkle below

there is nothing for me here
i have clawed the wallpaper
to ribbons
brought down the ceiling upon my head

the vase is broken,
the ground is nourished

what was wide has closed
the mouth is pinned closed
and the seat is of the high heavens

the wheel is bound up with
frayed ribbons and all of
the men
have been called up for war

there are pieces of coloured pottery
between my hands
the river picked clean

the vase is broken,
this is still my home

# Khorovod

the evil will be endless:
a bristling light,
a sinner's finger,
a blue finger

pushed through the earth.
where can we go
from here?
*only where they send us.*

what shall we see?
*we shall see nothing.*
the man has changed
colour under the sunlight.

he has turned from
purple to yellow,
he has seen the glow
of the moon

behind the sun's halo
and she has gazed back.
the *babushka* was
frozen stiff in her

own garden, the cat's
head swelled and dropped
off as it slept by the
window.

the evil flows out
from the land, not from
the sky. in our village
there is putrefaction

before death. when
we remove our gloves
the skin of our palms
comes with them.

there is a *khorovod*
danced by girls with bubbling,
shaking knees in a field
to the north –

they will appease the land,
or it will swallow us whole.

# The Monk

in the garden, each budding stem holds a ring of
blood between cupped hands. the wind whispers
its prayers across the fingertips, the canopy
is vaulted and ribbed high above.

the bowerbird counts its rosary in the
shrubbery, tearing apart the heads of
cornflowers and reassembling them in the
form of something divine. the sky is pinned

on all sides by pillars of iron, a cloth
held in place by metal and heat, but nestled
within this cloister all is peaceful, all is
silent. dawn extends its rosy fingers

and grasps the clouds, wringing the water from
them and scattering it to encrust every blade
of grass, every leaf blurred by the twilight.
breath by breath, the garden folds into

life, and the first bloom lifts its head
from a night of contemplation.

# The Hatchling

a bird hatched today in the crook
of the birch tree:
soft and veined,
spun like fine silk
from the silvered cup of albumen,

pale and frothing,
milky-eyed, yawning,
rolling, slug-like, a
glistening bead of
burnished ire,

born and swaddled in
the bandages of the
scarred birch tree,
kept warm between
a mother's hands.

the clouds gathered their
black cloth and cast it
down upon the earth,
a storm unfurled, the sky pinched
and creased, glistening with
tyrian purple, spilling pillars
of molten silver

to pierce and drench

the woodland, the leaves
shuddered, the nest tossed
and the hatchling

flopped out onto the ground
far below, struggled, could
not raise even its head above the

brown plateaus of leaf litter
or the thick, dripping
stubby shoots of ferns.

the mother, her dark feathers
shifting against the purple light
of the gathering storm, the wind
lifting and
dropping her in turn,

flew down from the nest,
watched the hatchling struggle,
pink and wet in the undergrowth,

watched with her shining eye,

and a breath later,
as the wind stilled,

the mother bird devoured
her baby in pieces,

weeping all the while.

# The Temple Garden

The temple garden bursting to life:
buds reddening on their branches
and turning to thin, fibrous leaves,

The pit into which the bird flew
covered over with the first flowers
of the year, sprinkled with blessed

water and then sealed shut, the
place of worship veiled in the silver
cowl of Springtime.

Only the priest, who tends the sacred
garden, is aware of them. He burns
incense while he cuts

Wreaths for the freshly-cleaned altar,
and steps carefully, moves his fingers
with the grace of a stork's leg

so as not to crush them. Far from him,
they huddle under a leaf, overturned
and browning. Here, they pray,

They form their own circle, give water,

drawn from a pool in the crook of a stone
that they named sacred, in offering

to Gods no larger than a house-cat.
They capture beetles and make
sacrifice of them, screaming and dancing

to songs no human ear could hear.
The priest knows of them, for he
has seen them scurrying about the place,

Leaping from flower to flower, stealing
spider-webs to spin their clothing,
gazing into a dewdrop in wait of

a vision from the most mighty.
The priest knows of the tiny people
who live in the garden,
small enough to sleep

upon a fingernail,
but he speaks not.

# Vulparia

sweet nectar of round,
calm face:
yellow syrup from your
bright eye is skimmed from
a pool of gold, dripping upwards
into the red mound in
the corner, your warm
coagulation,
sipped by flies.

*look how you've grown* –
you are a prophet of my own feelings!
as if you can sense the
leaf, the twig about to be
placed on the stack,
you take your place
not on my lap but off to
the left somewhere,
close but distant –
there, right there!

there is where the
sleep turns to walking,
the twang that nobody
else can feel

opens outwards and blooms
like the colour of a cats eye,
the yellow prong
of *vulparia*,
the syrup-haunt on the air.

# The Walking-Bird

We cross the river, ourselves whole
and shimmering in the light cast from
the centre of the cloud. We sit in rigid
silence and we watch as the bird crosses

        the river,
his legs as two long fire-pokers gathering
the deep, reaching down with his hands
and trapping water within his vessel,
the

*dosing-vase*, the painted instruction.
We, leant towards starlight, will speak his
words:
        find the part where the bone is broken
        and press down
as hard as you can.

Allow the sensation to push its way
throughout your body, and cry for certain
that you are going to die.

Take yourself to the river and watch
the bird spill his remedies from his arms.
the women carrying their husbands in woven baskets

pass by here,

the village folk with their vivid,
painted masks hook the wind and
reel it in.

       Press again upon the broken bone.
Return to us.

# Hellebore

Along the riverbank the bodies rest:
eight of them, their heads smashed with hammers.
This is not a beautiful place. Did you
think this would be a beautiful place?

A serene spot to watch the water move,
to watch the birds drift along the surface,
fixed in place by a pressure from below,
moving without force; did you think you

would find peace here? Solace?
Rest? The only rest in this place is
for the dead. Their heads were smashed with
hammers, and they were dragged here

and left in the wet mud. They have
been here long enough that the earth
has begun to mould itself around their bodies,
and their sweetness leeches into the
water.

I saw barbarians marching across the grassland.
I saw eight men and women,
bleeding and bright in the grass.
This is not a beautiful place.

### The Nature of the Earth

The Earth is full of wonder.

I felt it beating when listening to a shell before it exploded –

Then my eyes perceived human heads, pressed together to form rock.

a beautiful primordial seascape :

a battle ending in a kiss :

A mouth around which the earth turns.

Some very beautiful women crossing a river and crying,

But now the strangulation is at its peak,

your victims caught up in the gears of violent stars come back to life

one wondered how he had managed to stick his head back on.

Wheel of Light.

### A Rock Garden in the sea

First morning, last morning, the world begins.

their skin became the crust, with giant mountains and hollows.

The rains came, and ran down into the hollows to make the oceans, swamp and thicket,

The Invisible Isle

a shoot of the Romantic tree, The stem branched in repeated forks.

The visual representation of a walking man cut in half :

homo sapiens, says he

Homo sapiens: we are warm blooded, kidney-shaped masses

'Sow your children in the corner of a wood . . .'

I have made myself a seer.

my vision: The exploding mountain buried the garden with ash and dust, killing two thousand people.

A string found on my table made me see a number of young people trampling their mother, or squashing two flies

## II. Summer - *The Augur*

# Cornfield Annuals

a bright flash and a blue flower,
livestock tamed and reared under the curling sun.
we rang in the cornfields like cotton-bells,
sang like hunters with their horns,
torn and scattered upon the ground.


a bright flash and a blue flower,
a stinger plunged under the skin by a
striped hand, the bloom and swelling
of purple flesh. The slowness of
the body, the weight of limbs held
fast by a spiral cut into a seed-pod –
here now,        gone now,
flickering along the surface of the world,


a bright flash and a blue flower,
the blackness behind your eyelids spotted with an iridescent, trembling colour.
i remember the days pulled from the calendar,
the months folded between palms,
crumpled or shredded by cruel fingers,
a life collapsing in on itself in all        places,
all moments. without contempt,
without passion i will not forget the light that blazed for only a second –


a bright flash and a blue flower

hanging from its stem and shifting like the rays of the moon,
strings whirling about a pale stone and then flopping down
through the damp canopy of a distant rainforest
filled with strange, long-snouted and reddened creatures,
all slumbering under a latticed window.

a bright flash and a blue flower,
a mirror broken over a compost heap
for the men who toiled in the cracked mud.
a feeling like a white, gauzy curtain flicking and glowing in a june breeze:

a bright flash,
a blue flower
and the sun above the cattle.

# The Dance of the Sun

the rulers of the
      wasteland,

   the ridged
hum of a mesa banded with
   thick slabs cut from the thigh of
   a sacrificial bull,
   the golden-horned
                    *Sun*

twisting her dance across the sky,
ruffled skirts aflame,
      turning to dust with
      a vicious scream.

            the vastness,
            the desolation of this place
has much to say.
voices quiver on the ends
of stems dried and bleached, tilting in the
light breeze, and you listen.

this, the endless iron-red landscape
or the scraped pit of the sky:
                        this is the dwelling-place
                        of God.

# Fire on the Grassland

I saw it up there
only for a moment:
the sky flashed red,
hot with flame,

and then began to fall around
me. I pushed my hands
against the dry earth,
felt the hum of
neuron and spine below me,

the caress of warm
breaths passing each other by,
the house filling up with sand,
the bird    cut apart.

I acted without reason,
without thought. I pushed
a glass across a table,
I forgave all sins,
I tore

my ear off and
threw it into the fire.
I knew, and became

what I knew.
I betrayed the work of years,
spoke freely, moved as though my
legs were bound to metal rods.

I saw the flash of red
in the sky,
saw the clouds tangle,
tangled my fingers together and refused it,

or accepted,
I saw the sky clotted with blood,

and looked to the path behind me.

# Omphalos

I met you there on the bridge,
a mist thrown up around us by the silvered
blast of the waterfall, each breath a creak to
rock the aged wood. There were mighty vines

climbing the legs of trees, muscled like the
Python, heavy with frilled, spiralling flowers
with a scent that could cause flights of vision,
leaves that tumbled into the black abyss of

jungle far below. There we spoke, where none
but the water could hear us, and made our oath.
The terms did not matter, we knew – all that
was important was that a promise was made,

that my fate was lain before me at my feet,
bundled on a cushion of sponge-wet moss,
our vow a contortion in the sheet of Time,
a knot upon which to whet one's teeth.

When we swore our oath,
in the distance I heard the
bleak call
                of a black stork.

# Ritual of the Rival Tribes

the woman in the garden,
choked in a damp tangle of leaves.
here, the flower grows from the fruit,
and the dawn is within the hood of the monk.


the man, pinned by the arms and
dragged to the town square. the people
sing,
>'TRAITOR!
>TRAITOR!'
and crush him beneath a mound of stones.


at the place of execution, the scorched ground
is swept with a broom, a cloud of dust rising
like incense, scaled and bright in the sunlight –
a minaret begins to unfurl in the garden.


the clasped fingers and the blades of grass
form their dancing-circles, an idea is
shared in hushed voices in the corners of rooms,
the problem turned over in shaking hands.


the dead woman rises again,
and dances in the street.
the mesh of summer splits in two

and allows a bright red flame through –
a question is asked:

the answer is a blue flower dropped
into a cup of wine.

# Lake Svetloyar in a Rainstorm

Here, the bell chimes.
Here, the motion is stopped,

the breath catching behind my tongue,

the ground pulled from beneath him
as a silken scarf cast from the shoulders.

all sound flowed outwards from the place,
hot as blown glass,

and i looked
up towards the dark, swelling clot,
the cloudburst,

the throat of the storm
drawn back by flashes of

pearl-blue light,

the summer rain tearing sharp
through the flesh as

the man leapt from the tower.

Here, the bell chimes.
Here, the earth receives.

# Cataglyphis

The silence blinded me for a moment:
the glare of the sun, the banded mesa,
the bone-white flower upon the spiked
column that grew from the sand.

Here, where the earth shakes and
turns beneath our feet, where the
air itself is hot as fire, this is where
we shall build our temple.

Here we pray, and come to know
Divinity through searing heat.
Even the silvered ant, tilting
and shaking on the end of some

dried stalk, pausing for a moment
before returning to its home below
the earth, yes, even the ant sees
God in this place.

I touch a finger to my brow
and find water – there, swimming
in a holy well, basking
in the glory of the blazing

Silence above,
is my own self in bloom.

# A Feast For the Earth

i will show you this:
the heap upon stone,
the vein of red within the stone,
the red upon the stone, and
the restful, skyward gaze,
and you will say, *'how sad!*

*how sad the fate of that man,*
*bleeding beneath the sacrificial mound,'*
and i will let you say it, but i
will not hear it. this is a beautiful
thing, a wonder,
a blessing. in his death, the
man has become sacred,

given over to the Gods and
carried to a shining place, a joyful
place: the centre of the sun.

he was carried to the altar-stone by
the haruspex with his
cornflower-blue robe,
struggling, quaking,
pale ridge of muscle
framing the landscape of his skin,

the sand dunes lifting – up, down, up
again, fingers reaching,

delighted. the air bristled at the moment
the blade entered him, the barrel opened,
wine pouring forth, purple and fragrant,
the liver held aloft by stained hands. the
haruspex ran his hands along the organ,
received vision and spoke the words
written by the Gods upon the glistening pink,

and then left him at the flower-laden temple.
his flesh peeled into the air,
sloughed off in oozing,
steaming ribbons and carried away,
grazing the crown of the sun,
his body boiling as it turned the colour of hellebore,
a beauty, a wonder
crushed under the weight,

his bones frilled with decay:

a feast for the earth.

# Goodbye to Rubber Island

Come here with me now
across the bridge, behind
the curtain that glistens with dewdrops,

the gauze that shines
despite everything. We are
bound to this fate like a

dog rooted in the garden,
like a flower that showed its
curl to the sun for only

an hour before it became
flake and dust. Come with me
to milkweed-smell, to

the well that heals. The
circle, the wheel is all and
everything, and we are

pinned, with clutches of bloom,
to its centre.

# The Sibyl of the Rhine

when i came down,
a bird had flown into the kitchen:
howling,
shrieking, black-spotted wings flashing against the window,
omen of death,
the terror in listening.

the sky had split open,
jewels thrown into the hard soil.
i stood upon rolling glass
and knew that i would not fall,
watched the flowers bow and shake off water,
calm their lights against the earth –

when i came,
cold and sweat-drenched,
from the top of the hill,
they had summoned the Spirit from
the Holy Land and tied it between two seed-pods.
the heat remained in the woodland
long after the sun passed.

they have said to me,
*'why are you doing this?'*
yet i am so enamored by the

colour of the velvet, the blazing
sunlight trapped within your jewels,
the flame

at your heel, the dust that passes
through the wing-feathers.
the garden was split into halves
by breath
and turned to blue and red,
and i untied the rope,
felt the weight against my hands

when i came down,
i was impure before God

Oil runs still from the crushed man,
rose-glow, bloody fruit, flayed by the seasons;
a terrible cry of birds in his own skull.

cut stones, Bared bones,
the painted beasts' flourish
we might draw in the ash;
divining A way of living
Or death by cold fire
a dance of light against black rain;
coronet beneath cloud,

sky breaks open again and again
where the horizon was;

A rite.
Thirst is endless
And the pools run dry.

The city falls,
exploding in fireworks;

the old boundary burning
Yet never burned.

the aridity of an emptying world

Already the wind stirs

Nothing's undone or loosened here,

order is made.

I'll dream and wake untroubled.

III. Autumn - *The Haruspex*

# For Mother Deó

cut in a spiral
and oozing
milk,

droplets of pearl
falling against
soft garnet

the raging
bull's dance, the
throat torn open

as hands reach
to catch
the blood,

reddening the petals.

# The Folded Cloth

A *peeling back of layers*:
a view from overhead
of farmland, ranks of golden
barley and the meadow blackened
by ash.

The columbine, with its drooping head,
the poppy that holds the sun
between two mangled hands
and their bejewelled court
of flashing blooms,
tilting

as the land tilts below them. The
storm gathering above, pulling the
dust from their leaves and soaking
everything, bright and rigid.
The smile of the bearded clouds,

the *wideness of all that is*
and the layers peeled back:
the skin is torn from the sacrificial
bull to the frenetic calls of the
women with knotted hair.

And here, the stars held on sheets
of clear film, placed over one another.
This one a red mark left by many
millions of years, a spark thrown
from the fireplace
and then covered over
with endless strips of transparent fabric:

layers to be peeled back by
the hands of the diviner
after the piling-on of time.

# Bursting People

i was standing on the white ridge,
the stones flashing between patches of
blazing heather, watching the city, seeing
lights swell and smudge like droplets of
oil distorted by a ripple in the water.

i was gazing at a pool of water that had
formed between stems of grass,
watching the faces held within as they
bloomed, first turning a noble red and
then splitting down the middle, thick ruffles

of purple, grey and brown bursting and
shifting in the wind, shaking their fibres
like corals, like some lacy sea-creature
raising its fans towards the jarred sun to
sift its nourishment from the breeze.

here, the life comes from above as from
below, sinking on a slip of vermilion,
a strand tied about a cloud, measured with
gentle fingers and trapped, and cut –

i could only stand there watching as it
was weighed in the cup of a palm,

and all around,
the people burst
like the head
of a poppy.

# Woodlover's Paralysis

The man is at rest, the priestess told us.
He was carried into the temple by men
who bound their hands with silk, men
who would not touch his skin as it became
a revelry of flame,

The sharp heat of a bird that has not yet flown
the nest, howling, widening its mouth in
anticipation of a blessing from above, making
its pathway in the cavity of his chest. He is not
sleeping:

His eyes are as open as any, their narrow rings
of green swallowed by his pupils. He has the look
of one who has imbibed the sacred drink, who
has received the blessing of the forest-spirits and
seen their wealth

Stretch before him, all things carpeted in sapphires
and emeralds, the sky diamond-pale, cupped in shaking
hands. He is aware, hanging from the edge of the deep,
bellowing vase of slumber yet never falling in. He does
not move,

Cannot move – his limbs are as stiff as beams and every

part of him is glazed with sweat. The man's skin
is washed clean and made pale with terror. If he moves,
if he tries to lift his head – what will happen? There is
no question, he is sure of it:

The pain will flash across him in waves. He will
be flayed by the seasons. His skin will tear from him,
rich and delicious, his muscles exposed, kissed with the
cool blade of the wind. His fingertips will blacken with
the cold and his

Hands will drop from their sockets. A sensation will spread
along his arms and legs: they will be crushed as though
in a vice, and all he carries within him will be forced
through a single point. He feels he is in the body of the
man given at the Temple,

His head squeezed between stones, his liver torn from him
by stained hands. A warm, breathing garnet is held up
to the Sun and gazed into, and it is seen at once: if the
man were to move, yes, it is known,

He would die in agony.

# The Sacrifice

The pile of fruit
was taken and wrapped in
pale linen
And then laid in the woods
in a crook at the bottom
of a wide oak tree.

A swollen pomegranate
was crushed and spilled
its seeds across the
temple floor in the
height of the season.
A plum was plucked
from the branch and
skinned while it
dripped sweet red
nectar all into the earth,
glistening dewdrops or
hot, shining garnets
that sank into the mud.

The priests swung their
censers as they proceeded
through the woodland to
the site,

The fruits were picked at
by the crows and magpies
before they grew furred and
purple,

and turned into long
strands of bone.

# Persephone

the syrup, the sweetness of the fruit is yours for life.
it swells and reddens before falling from the tree, and
grows even as you hold it.

you take a bite, and then another, and you do not stop
until your mouth is full and bleeding.
you are ravenous. you would chew off

your own hands if they had been coated with honey.
when you eat, you become a dog with its legs broken –

thoughts become shrunken, become blackened, become covered.
*the mind is as a stone rolling down a hill.*

all things twist and bend, then collapse into a web of colour.
your teeth snap
from the root
and float from your mouth.

the world quickens and blushes
and birds hang upside-down from a cloud
while your eyes clatter about in your head.

you bite, you chew, you feel the branching stem.

                              you revere and pray to
                              the feeling of surrender.

# Apotropaia

Against pestilence that
creeps and presses itself close to
the rooftops, the windows,

Against the clawed hand
that snatches at the pearl as it
tumbles through the reeds,

Against the demon and
the dancing woman, I will
protect myself.

With this magic I shall be guarded
from fowler's snare or twisting adder,
from the lapis-dyed flame of

Monkshood or the rocky
outcrop far beneath the cliff
I will leap from – here,

Tilt your ear this way and
hear us witches –

    *we demand to be safe.*

# Mourning

you, with your syrup-bright eyes,
asleep in a sunbeam, fur shifting tones,
burnt and stained, then vivid and bright,
a yawn rocking through your body,

limbs pushed out as far as they could go,
and then without motion again, the strings
cut, sending you into deep sleep. We searched
for you for weeks. You were lost to us,

flattened under some wheel or washed away by
the rain, sunk into the pit of a rank of young fuchsias.
I dreamt that you were taken by a fox, torn
to pieces, the grass sweetened with your

blood and sinew. I felt my sense of you sever,
pulled behind a gauze, and saw instead a hillside
stitched with heavy flowers ripe for unpicking
by a tiny claw. I had other dreams, too,

ones where you returned to us one day,
slipping through the cat flap and shaking off
the rain, stealing your fill of biscuits
and finding a sunny window to nap in as though

you'd never left.

# An Ear of Grain in Silence Reaped

See how it is now –
    the dappled wreath, black-spotted with fungus,
    a marking on the neck
of  the outsider. See how we love beneath the lime-tree,

see how our bodies are tied with rope,
    pressed fl ush against  one another,
    bristling and        ridged,
catching
           the sunr ise in our web.

If I must, I will turn your head and make you see.
    Is it not beautiful? Are you not aflame with joy?
    Touch now the pale flower, turn it red.
*There* are many things that can be done, and many things

      you will affect without awareness of your own impact.
See now how your weight bends the threads,
 how you may alter all  you come into contact with.
The river's mouth yawns just    beyond those hills

there, do you see them? and in the crook of the valley,
that   place:    *that* is where we will bind   our own
        selves to the stake
        and dissolve, soul and body both,
                into flame.

# The Weight, the Desolation

boats are moored in dark water,
the river still as glass.
no one is here.
the rain pools in the cup of a
flower,
released moments later by the
bowing of heads.

under the earth, a mound is growing,
ridged and bumped,
bursting through redness,
amniotic,
pure as cloud.
no one is here.
the mound rises high,
shows its feathered underbelly
and turns to black oil.

no one is here.
no one passes through this place:
the canopy covers the sun,
cuts bright gold across the earth.
the desert of a leaf
decays into nothing more than skeleton.
no one is here.

a bird rises into the air,
making no sound.
a squirrel casts itself from the branch,
silent,
unable to cut through
the grey membrane.
a swell moves beneath the water,
a boat quivers,
the surface shimmers,
but nothing is heard,

no one has come.

A dark place,
a quiet sun.

In the frozen soil,

The *Spring-bird* waits.

IV. Winter - *The Wanderer*

# Rite of Passage

The wind said

*take care not to spill the water,*

the wind said

*gaze not upon the face.*

The wind said

*breathe in the ash, and be free,*

the wind said

*peel open your skin to welcome the rain.*

The wind said

*everything has its place.*

# Sepulchre

I find my peace here,
in a wet crag by the sea,
the very land pulsing with the
rhythm of the waves,

the heave of a black landscape
pressing itself against the stones.
I rest, curled against salt-worn
stones and thick wreathes of

gelatinous seaweed hauled up
by the tide. Here, I am hidden from
dark eyes and bright ones,
no voice carries here, no call,

no sound. In this small place of mine,
in this shelter, I am safe.
As the water begins to pool around my feet,
I am safe.

I feel a ring of cold travel up my body,
and know that I am safe here.
I look now to the sky, jagged with cloud,
grazed and purple like a carcass

dragged across the shore.

*I let the wave take me.*

# Patterned Silence

the cat scratches behind
her ear without moving.
the harp plucks its own
string, and then becomes
silent.

*now is a time for peace.*

the light has passed, and
now the sky is cut with
blue and red bars.
under the ground, a root
twitches its finger,
making stem and
leaf thick with water.

*now is a time for peace.*

the dawn is filled with
sound, but no one hears
it. a grain of dust grows
legs and walks away, and
the air hangs still above
the table. nothing can
move. nothing can stir.

a whale is frozen inside
a sapphire, its calf
hanging in a moonbeam.
the waves take a welcome
rest from beating against
the cliffs. all life crawls
out from a flat plane
of grey, and then crawls
back in again.

68

# Injuries are Omens

asleep in bed,
solid,
shapeless.
in pursuit
or tied
by one hand with an unseen rope.

burning on the moorlands,
redeeming yourself in
the eyes of God. you pull off
your skin and fill your mouth
with speckled moss.

drowning in this dream,
hot and lurid, swollen like the
bank of a frozen lake –
a bird calls
and your body convulses:

you fall through the bed,
solid,
shapeless.

standing in a river
that runs through the house,

your eyes tilting back in their
sockets. you stare into a
flame, watch it grow outwards

and then pull itself apart
into a single long thread.

a Russian woman starved to death
inside a shoebox she convinced
herself she could never exit.
a man tore out his fingernails
to spite his face.
you licked the man's  palm
and viewed yourself
from across the room,

falling through the bed.

# The Dance of the Earth

the wind stirs,
and the land lifts and flutters
like a sheet of white
cotton, clean and fragrant,

a veil of ice disturbed by
deft fingers, flicking water
into the crease between
the hilltops,

letting it pool, the fog
a cream-smear upon the
dale: gentle, fresh, the
spires of frost

slithering into the air,
the crushed blade of
grass, the space
where the stork lands,

breathing spirals of
warm mist, claws dark
and clutching at the
snow. a bead of water

swells at the bud-wound,
glistens, a scrying-cup,
full, bursting with vision,
satiating the prophets:

the *Walking-Bird* bothering
its feathers, tilting sharp
head on its stem, the Earth
shimmering, hardened with
death, the stork

folding the burial shroud
and sweeping away the
sun

# Libation to the Potamoi

the gold of the flame is temptation,
the thick wax of the river spilled over its banks
and held between the warm hands of the valley.

waiting for the dust to settle,
gripping our ears until they redden,
eyes pressed to the windows.

the shimmer spread across the land,
a wreath hung from the trees that stand
perfectly aligned with one another,

rising from the water, walking along the surface.
watching for the radiant debris to fall
along the roofs of our houses, the city

in flames, the swollen river
and the jewelled temptation.

# Urticaria

trees
ribbed, vein-like
and splintering
vein-line
beneath skin,
we are
moving beneath
the water,
made apocryphal:
a woman is standing in the road
and her shadow has become water.

i reach down into
the mire and find a
nettle – flowering,
white
explosive
hoods uncurl,
the head of the
dog of the monk –
and touch it,
not with fingers but with light
and the light
is split apart by the mud
and split apart by the

water,
the bright mire,
the      *Pure Land* and the
woman's shadow,
the light        is scattered
like the ray-arms
of   trees.

# Pyroclast

the ocean tears in two
and from its paper,
an island rises, red and frothing,
built around a funeral pyre.

a ship is tossed by a great wave,
shedding its skin, freeing itself.
a man sobs, bound to the mast,
and proclaims that which he has seen.

milk-flowers and glaring hellebores
are forming and pushing
their tongues through the earth
along the path,
the long way home.

a wanderer in the desert reaches
into his nose and pulls out
a living bird, painted and glorious.
he bites into it without a thought.

the water heaves and quivers,
the glowing island reaches a
black, bulbous finger skywards
and shatters a glass ball.

# The Warm Coil of God

the world is full of beautiful things:
i heard it when lifted the twisted shell to my ear,
listened for it rolling along the waxed-pink hill.
yes, the world and all within it has beauty and is beautiful.

the sand-dunes with their wisps of blackened grass
are a landscape made sacred, the great silver-tipped shafts
of rain that turn beneath the moonlight
are spears of divine radiance sent to awaken the land by way of impalement.

the pit where my finger joins my palm is the place the cattle will
be sacrificed, their limbs tied with lengths of rope. the hell, and the mouth
of hell – the libation is poured upon the hand and the shrinking
of the flame is the very coil of *God*.

the world is full of beautiful things:
i heard it beating when i raised the shell to listen,
heard it at the moment i opened my eyes as wide as they could go
and received
as the clouds parted.

# The Black Stork

the herald of spring:
a striding bird
or golden coin,
cutting through the water.

the dreaming man
in the dream-state,
he who crosses the veil,
a stone skittering along the border.

we assemble for the rite, feeling the breath
of the *bird* upon the tips of our fingers:
the earth grows warm, the bruised purple
bud of the hellebore emerging, swollen with dew,
through the soil as the sky reddens and an eye
begins to open.

the dancers gather up their
skirts now, the boys raise
flutes to their lips, a hymn for
the endless steppe.

as the land awakes, the stork
flutters his wings: up,
and then down, a black
flash

and a wheel slowly turning.

## ABOUT THE AUTHOR

James Rance is a poet, collage artist, and performer based in York, North Yorkshire. His poetry takes inspiration from Pagan spirituality and dreams, delving into previously unexplored aspects of the self for examination and analysis. Influenced by surrealism, imagism, psychedelia, and the slightly absurd, his work aims to give the reader strange sensations and vivid emotion. His collages have been used as cover art for several Acid Bath Publishing books and he frequently performs his poetry at events hosted by *Forge Zine* and York Howlers open mic poetry nights. His previous work has been published by Valley Press and York Centre for Writing, Greenteeth Press, Pilot Press, and elsewhere. Find him on Instagram: @james.rance48

## MORE BY JAMES RANCE

*Bagworm* (Greenteeth Press)

## ABOUT THE PUBLISHER

Acid Bath Publishing is an independent publishing house founded in Sheffield in May 2020. We are dedicated to publishing fiction and poetry that is clear, candid, and corrosive.

Contact us by email at
acidbathpublishing@gmail.com.

## ALSO FROM ACID BATH PUBLISHING

*Wage Slaves: An Anthology of the Underemployed*
*The Worst Best Years: A Student Life Anthology*
*Travels and Tribulations*
*Welcome Back, Frank* by N.J. Foley
*A Pocket Anthology of Addiction & Recovery*